We Like the Park

by Selina Lin
illustrated by Shirley Ng-Benitez

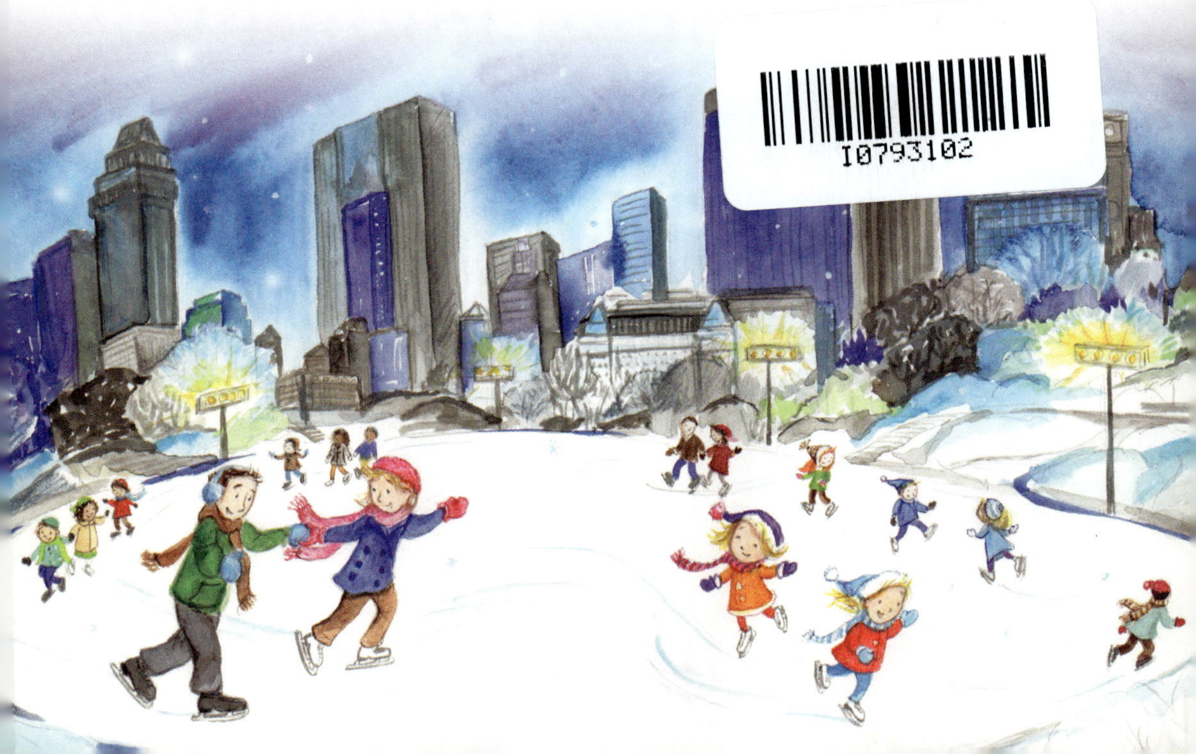

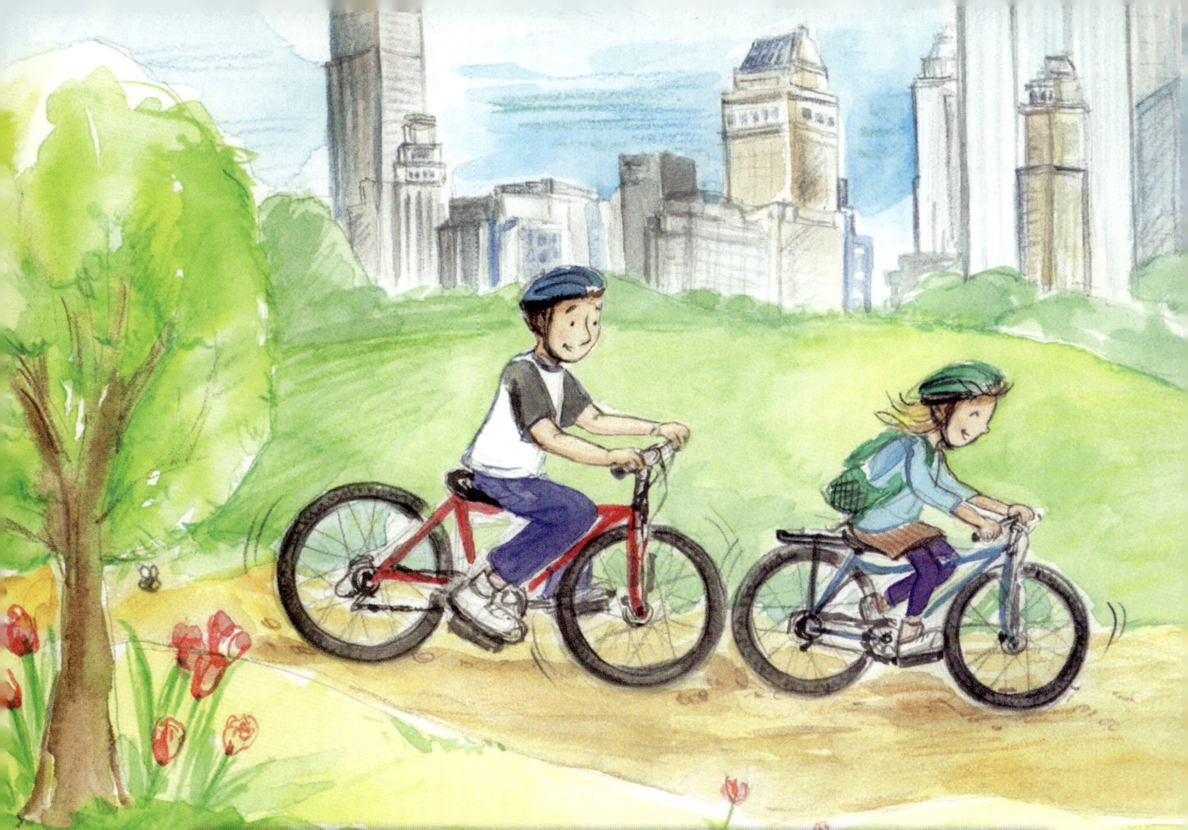

We like to 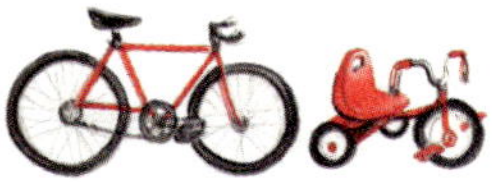 ride bikes.

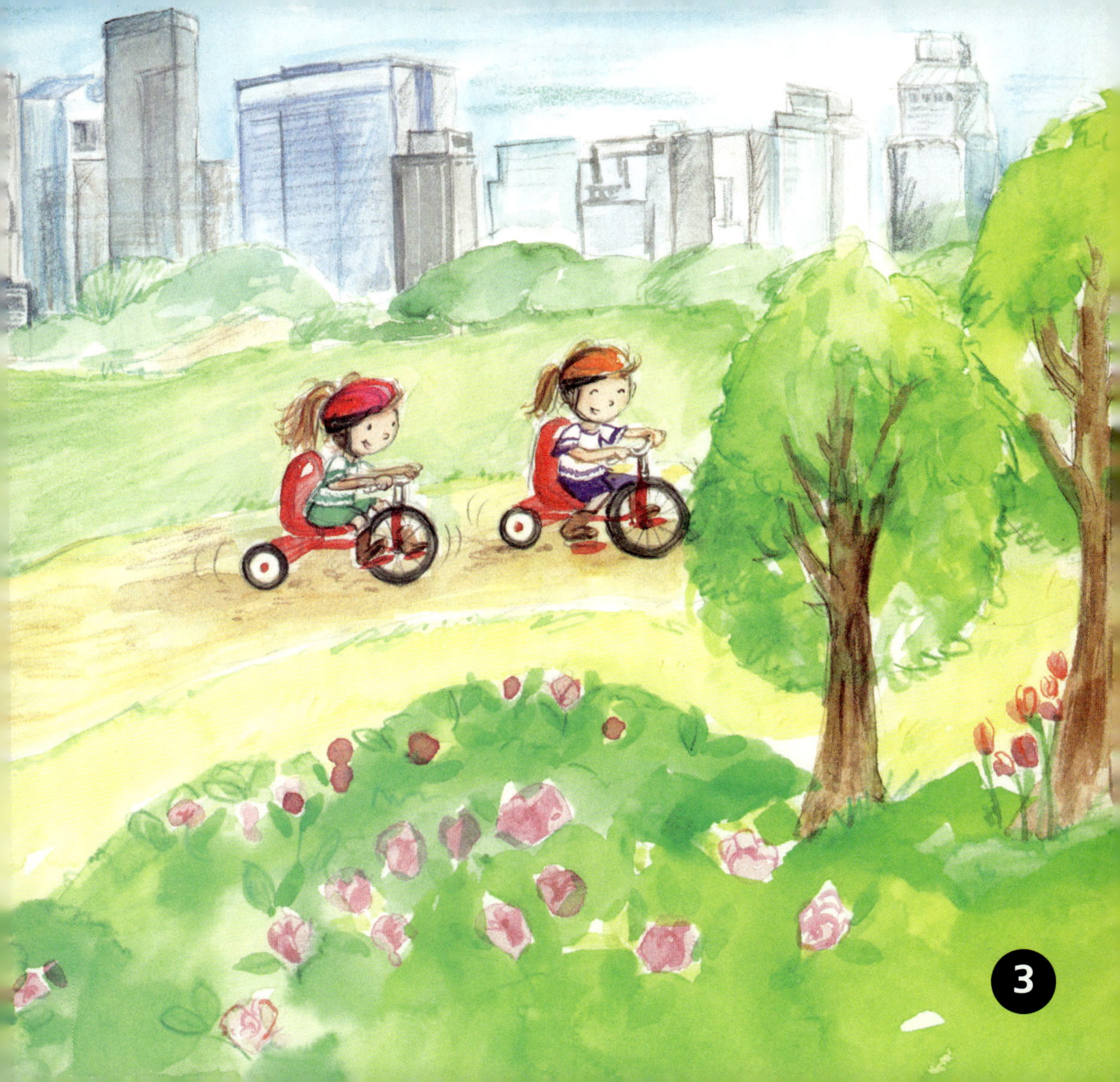

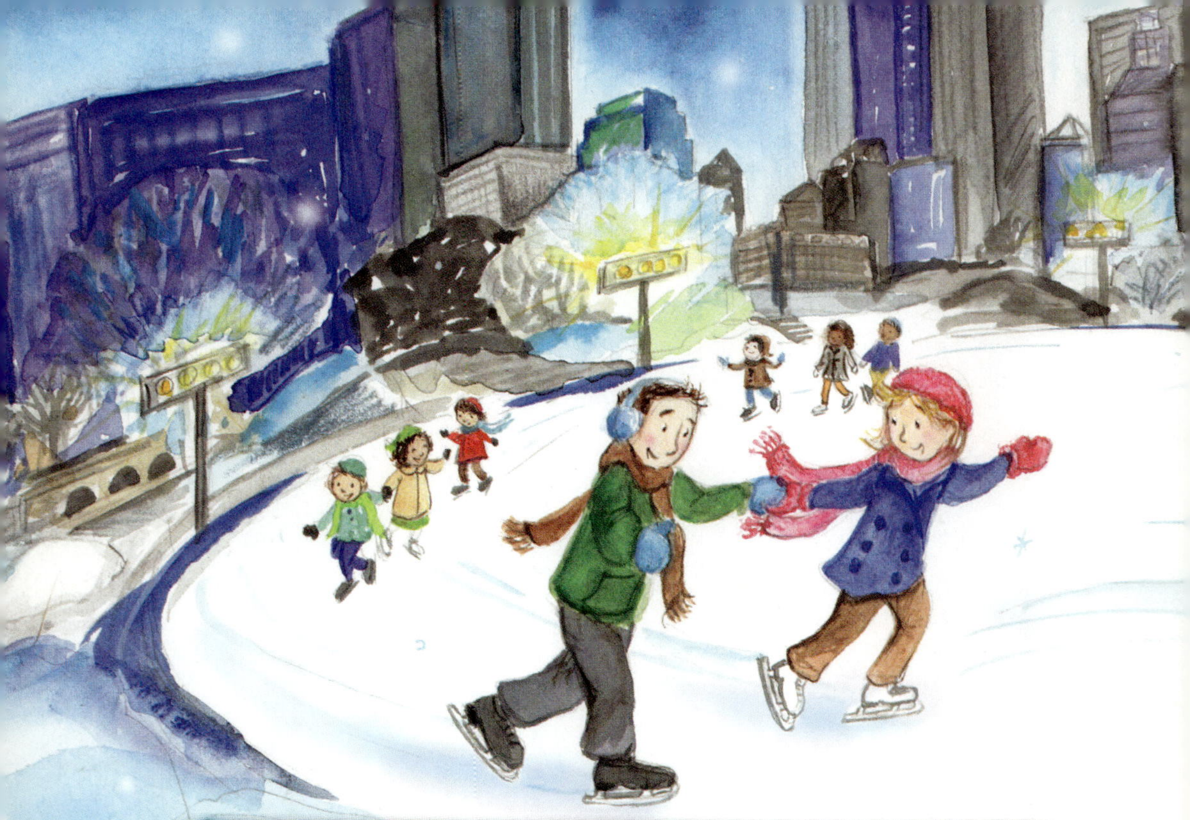

We like to 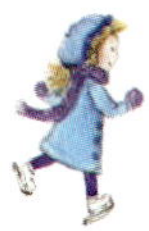 ice skate .

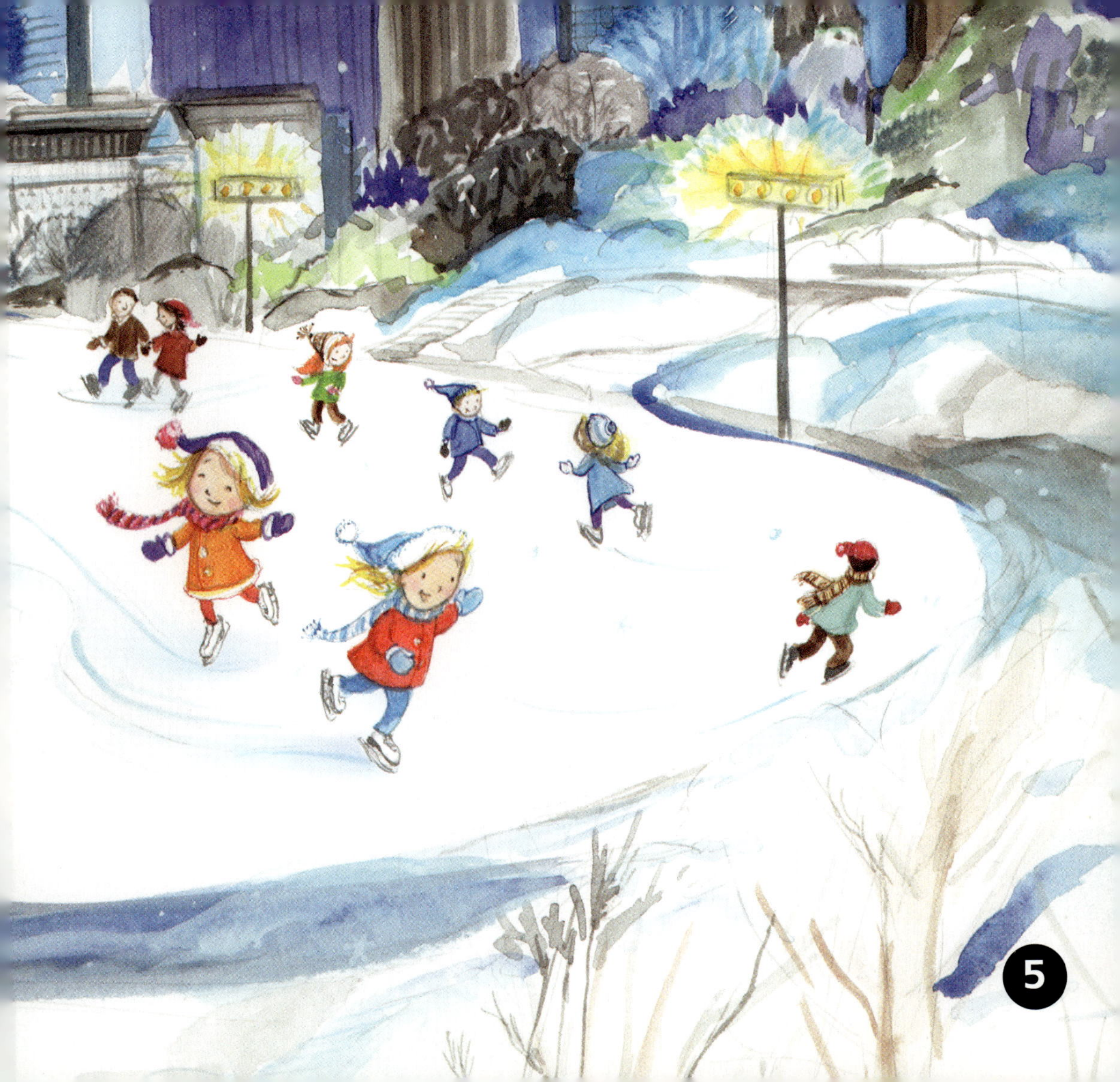

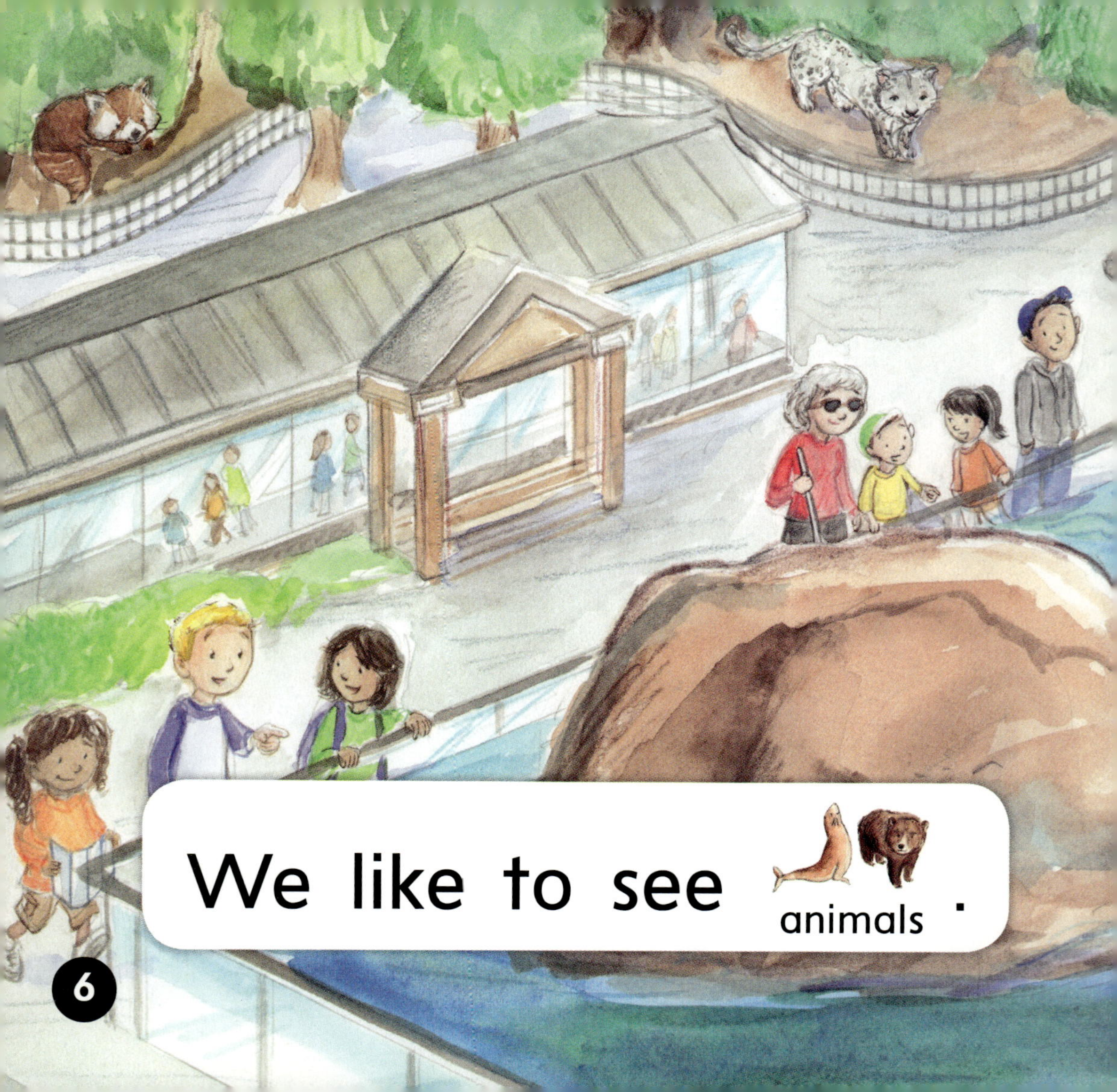

We like to see animals .

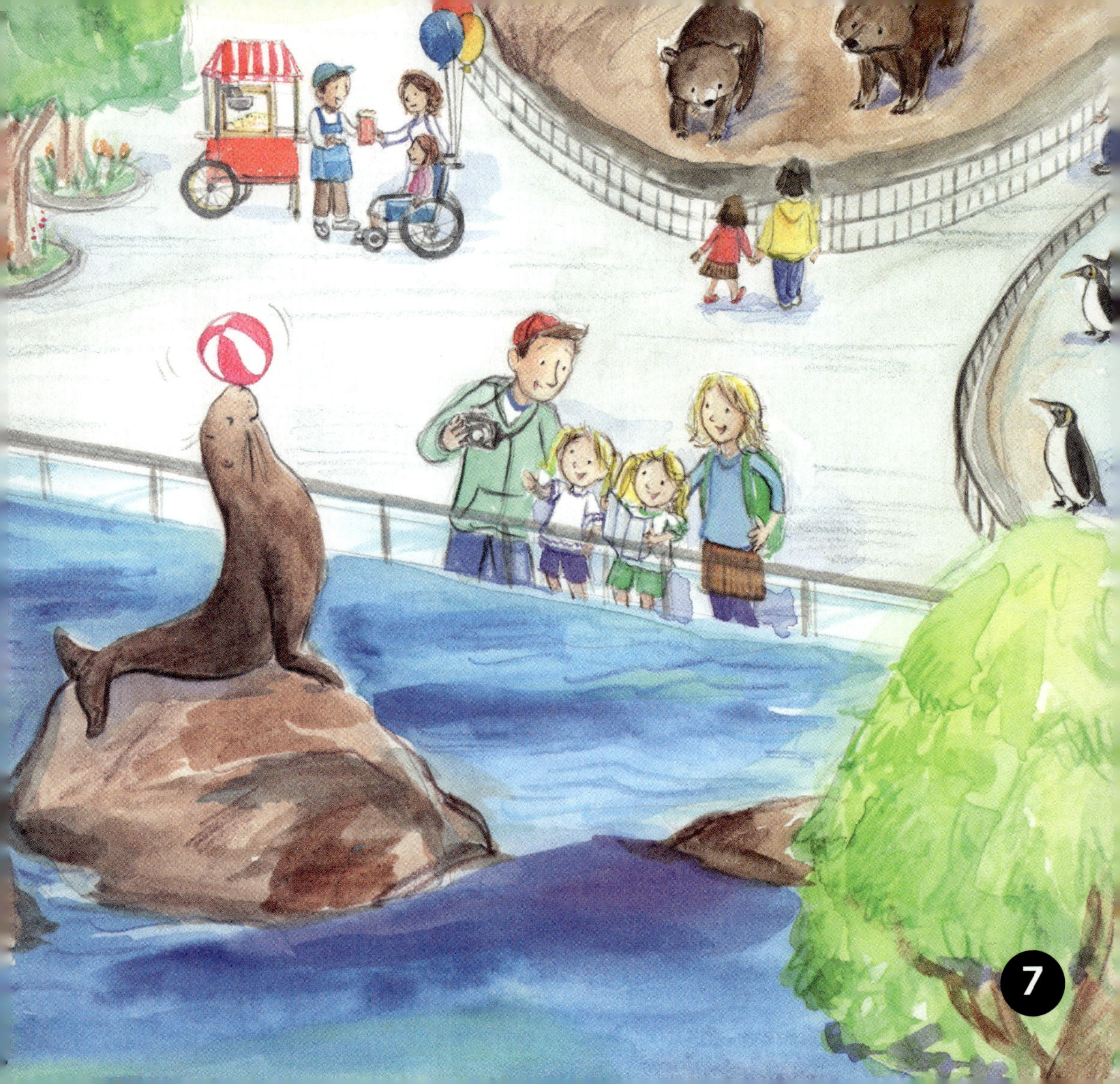

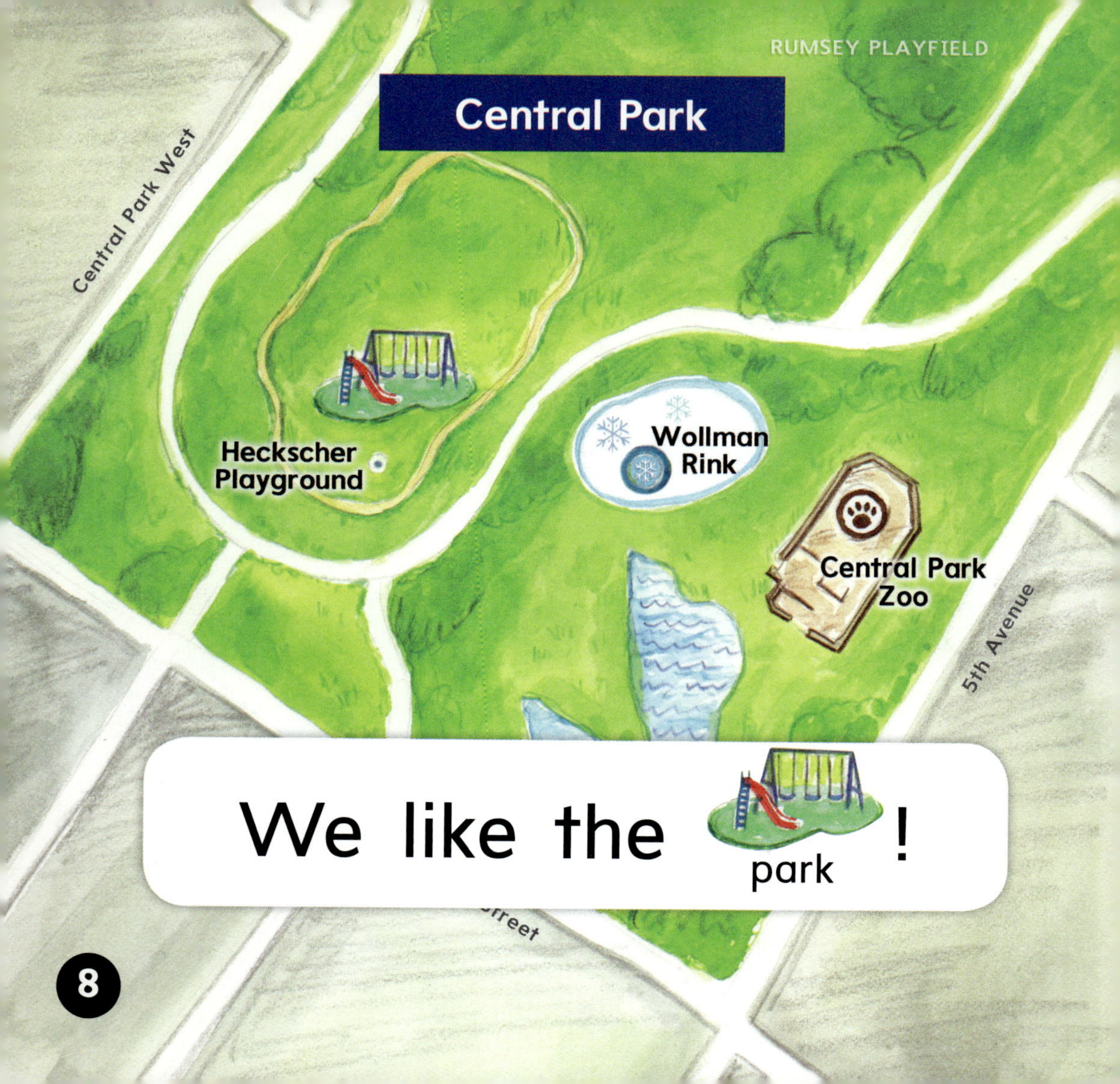

We like the park!